Glass Bead Making

Preparation - *Silica powder and soda ash are mixed with coloring agents.*

Liquefaction - *The mixture is melted in a kiln for about 20 hours at 1300°F.*

Tube Making - *In a kiln, glass is pulled into long thin shapes while air is blown into the center to form long tubes.*

Cutting - *The tubes are cut to approximate bead size by a blade spinning at extremely high speed.*

First Baking - *Cut pieces are placed in a 700°F rotating kiln to form round beads.*

Cleaning - *Beads are washed.*

Finishing - *Beads are heated in an electric kiln and polished to a high shine. Then various processes – coloring, lustre finishes, metallic finishes – are applied to the beads to enhance their beauty.*

Features of Toho Beads

Large Holes - *The size of the holes in Toho beads allows for threading multiple strands of thread or thicker thread, increasing the variety of beadwork you can achieve.*

Light Weight - *The larger hole means less weight so you get more beads when you buy by weight. There are approximately 111,800 size 11 Toho beads per kilo.*

Toho Triangle Beads　　　　**Toho Small & Large Round Beads**

Cylinder Bead Color Conversion Chart

Delica	Toho Treasure	Delica	Toho Treasure	Delica	Toho Treasure	Delica	Toho Treasure
141	A-1	420	A-553	325	A-705	76	A-781
201	A-121	417	A-554	324	A-706	58	A-782
234	A-145	410	A-557	327	A-710	86	A-783
51	A-161	35	A-558	21	A-711	74	A-785
100	A-162	412	A-559	31	A-712	80	A-786
179	A-176	413	A-560	38	A-713	1	A-81
41	A-21	414	A-561	32	A-714	2	A-82
42	A-22	421	A-562	34	A-715	7	A-83
22	A-221	422	A-563	351	A-761	3	A-84
22L	A-221A	423	A-564	352	A-762	4	A-85
44	A-23	451	A-601	353	A-763	5	A-86
62	A-241	452	A-602	354	A-764	6	A-88
87	A-245	455	A-605	355	A-765	233	A-903
43	A-25	310	A-610	56	A-771	235	A-906
200	A-41	306	A-611	85	A-773	244	A-909
104	A-425	301	A-612	59	A-774	246	A-910
124	A-457	307	A-613	60	A-775	243	A-917
135	A-461	311	A-617	63	A-776	238	A-920
10	A-49	33	A-701	66	A-777		
411	A-551	322	A-702	70	A-779		
418	A-552	312	A-703	72	A-780		

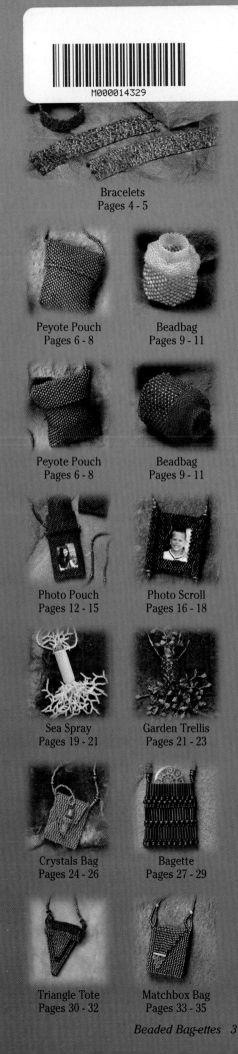

Bracelets
Pages 4 - 5

Peyote Pouch
Pages 6 - 8

Beadbag
Pages 9 - 11

Peyote Pouch
Pages 6 - 8

Beadbag
Pages 9 - 11

Photo Pouch
Pages 12 - 15

Photo Scroll
Pages 16 - 18

Sea Spray
Pages 19 - 21

Garden Trellis
Pages 21 - 23

Crystals Bag
Pages 24 - 26

Bagette
Pages 27 - 29

Triangle Tote
Pages 30 - 32

Matchbox Bag
Pages 33 - 35

As you follow these step-by-step instructions, you'll be learning the basics of the peyote stitch and making a charming and stylish bracelet. The peyote stitch is very versatile and is used extensively in beadwork.

Bracelet width is 1¼".

Teal Bracelet

Materials: 3 Black glass 6mm disk beads • Size B beading thread • Size 12 beading needle
Toho Beads
• 1 gram 11/0 round matte Gun Metal #611
Mix the following beads together:
• 7 grams 11/0 triangle matte Gun Metal #611
• 7 grams 11/0 matte Raku Gray/Green Iris #613
• 4 grams 11/0 triangle Metallic Hematite #81
• 7 grams 11/0 triangle matte Raku Teal/Plum Iris #706

Brown Bracelet

Materials: 3 Black glass 6mm disk beads • Size B beading thread • Size 12 beading needle
Toho Beads
• 1 gram 11/0 round matte Gun Metal #611
Mix the following beads together:
• 7 grams 11/0 triangle matte Soft Brown #702
• 7 grams 11/0 triangle matte Gun Metal #611
• 7 grams 11/0 matte Raku Gray/Green Iris #613
• 4 grams 11/0 triangle Metallic Hematite #81

Penny Bracelet

Materials: 3 Black 6mm disk beads • Size B beading thread • Size 12 beading needle
Toho Beads
• 1 gram 11/0 round Bronze Copper #222
• 25 grams Gold Luster Light Raspberry #202

About the Illustrations

Although you will be working primarily with triangle beads, the illustrations will be made with round beads. Treat the triangle beads just like you would round beads. Don't worry about how they are positioned as you work. Keep a consistent tension allowing for a little play and they will fall dutifully and randomly into place as they should.

Peyote Stitch #1

Row 1 - Pour a few triangle beads into a small shallow bowl or beading tray. Cut a 48" length of thread. Thread the needle with one end. Thread 16 triangle beads onto it and slide them down to within 6" of the other end.

Row 2 - Add the first bead as shown in Illustration 1.

Continue to add beads as shown in Illustration 2. Notice how the beads from the first row "share" the space with the new beads? Try to adjust your tension so that the row looks like Illustration 3.

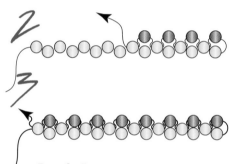

Row 3 - Reverse direction.
Add the first bead of the row as shown in Illustration 4. The completed row is shown in Illustration 5.

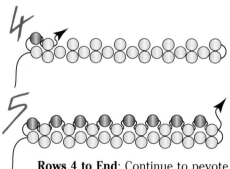

Rows 4 to End: Continue to peyote stitch rows as described above until the bracelet is the desired length.

Let's face facts - You're going to run out of thread at some point, but there's no need to panic – or to tie a knot! To end a thread, weave up and down through a few beads on the rows below. Clip thread end. Cut 36" length of thread and weave up and down through a few beads to come up out of the last bead you added. Weave down to end a thread, weave up to start a new one as shown in Illustration 6.

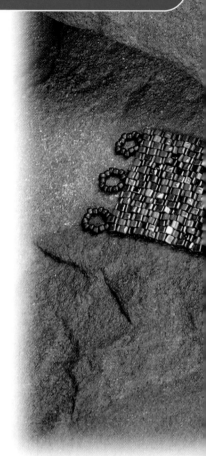

Weave up through several rows to start a new thread.

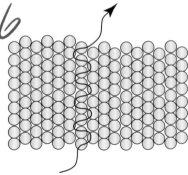

Secure Tail. Thread the needle with the beginning 6" tail of thread and weave it through several rows of stitching to secure. Clip thread close.

Let's make the loops. Thread needle with 36" of thread and weave it through several rows of stitching, eventually bringing the needle out through the bead shaded in gray on the far left of Illustration 7. This is where you will make the first bead loop.

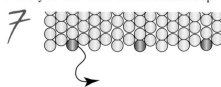

String 12 seed beads and bring the needle back through the left side of the gray bead as shown in Illustration 8. Weave the needle through the last row of beads until you reach the second gray bead.

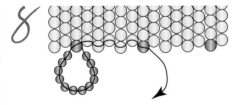

String 12 seed beads and bring the needle back through the left side of the shaded bead. Weave the needle through the last row of beads until you reach the third gray bead. Make another 12-bead loop as shown in Illustration 9. Weave the end of the thread along the long edge of the bracelet to the other side.

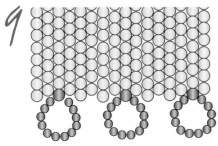

Now add the buttons. Weave the thread through the edge of the bracelet, bringing the needle out through the bead shaded in gray on the far left of Illustration 10. This is where you will add the first button.

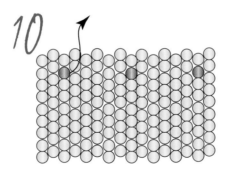

Thread a seed bead, a Black disk bead and another seed bead on needle. Pass the needle back through the disk and the first seed bead as shown in Illustration 11. Thread the needle back through the left side of the gray bead as shown.

Pull gently on the beads to bring them close to the rows of stitching. Not too close though, you'll need some play in order for the bead loop to hook under it. (It would be a good idea to go back through all the button beads a time or two to reinforce them.)

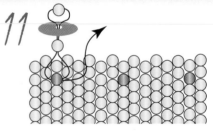

Weave through the edge of the bracelet, bringing the needle out through the second gray bead. Repeat the button process *(Illustration 12)*.

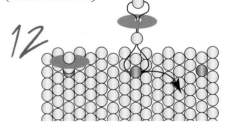

Weave through the edge of the bracelet and make another button at the third shaded bead. Weave the end of the thread through several rows of stitching to secure. Clip thread close.

You're done! Wear your snazzy new bracelet somewhere special. When people compliment you, smile sweetly and say "Thank You".

Create a stunning simple Peyote Pouch! The lid slides along the strap and closes securely creating a safe cache for a tiny treasure.

Peyote Pouch size is 1¹/₂" x 2".

Teal/Plum Pouch

MATERIALS: Size B beading thread • Size 12 beading needle
Toho Beads:
• 20 grams 11/0 round matte Raku Teal/ Plum Iris #706

Cabernet Pouch

MATERIALS: Size B beading thread • Size 12 beading needle
Toho Beads:
• 20 grams 11/0 round matte Cabernet #703

Brown Pouch

MATERIALS: Size B beading thread • Size 12 beading needle
Toho Beads:
• 20 grams 11/0 round matte Soft Brown #702

Bronze Pouch

MATERIALS: Size B beading thread • Size 12 beading needle
Toho Beads:
• 20 grams 11/0 round matte Soft Bronze #223F

The Big Picture

We'll be making the bag in two pieces – the body and the lid. Both pieces consist of a circular peyote stitch tube with a flat peyote stitch flap.

Peyote Stitch - #2

Row 1 - Pour a few seed beads into a small shallow bowl or beading tray. Cut a 48" length of thread. Thread the needle with one end. Thread 54 seed beads onto it and slide them down to within 6" of the other end. Pass the needle back through all of the beads again to form a circle *(Illustration 1)*. Bring the needle out just after the first bead strung. This way the tail won't interfere with the first few stitches!

Row 2 - Thread on a bead, skip the next bead in the row and thread the needle through the second bead *(Illustration 2)*.

Thread on another bead, skip the next bead in the row and thread the needle through the second bead *(Illustration 3)*.

Notice how the beads from the original circle "share" the space with the new beads? Try to adjust your tension so that the row looks more or less like Illustration 4. To keep the beads from twisting, hold the circle of beads between your thumb and forefinger. Continue adding beads in this fashion to the end of the row. (27 beads total)

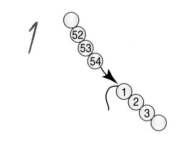

Row 3 - Do you see where your thread has come out of the last bead of Row 2? It's smack dab against the first bead of Row 2. This first bead is called the "step up" bead.

You have to "step up" through this bead to begin the next row *(Illustration 5a)*. You'll begin every row this way. As you can see in Illustration 4, the beads from Row 2 are higher than the rest. In Row 3 we'll place a bead in between each of these higher ones. Thread on a bead and pass your needle through the next high bead *(Illustration 5b)*. Continue adding beads in this manner to the end of the row (27 beads total).

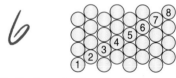

Rows 4 through 38 - This is the body of the bag. Step up at the beginning of each row, then add a bead between each of the beads from the previous row. You will be adding 27 beads on every row. Keep your tension consistent throughout.
Hint: To help you count the rows, count on the diagonal as shown in Illustration 6.

Let's face facts - You're going to run out of thread at some point, but there's no need to panic – or to tie a knot! To end a thread, weave up and down through a few beads on the rows below. Clip thread end. Cut 36" length of thread and weave up and down through a few beads to come up out of the last bead you added. Weave down to end a thread, weave up to start a new one *(Illustration 7)*.

Weave up to start a new thread.

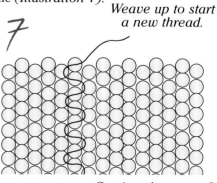

Continued on page 8

Row 39 - Now we're going to make a flat section that spans across the bottom of the bag. (The short sides of the bag bottom will be stitched to the flat section later.) Peyote stitch 11 beads.

Row 40 - Turn the bag over (from right to left). Add the first bead of the row as shown in Illustration 8.

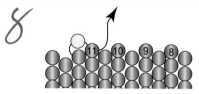

Continue to peyote stitch 10 more beads to finish the row.

Rows 41 through 43 - Turn the bag over, add the first bead of the row as shown in Illustration 8 and peyote stitch 10 more beads in each row *(Illustration 9)*.

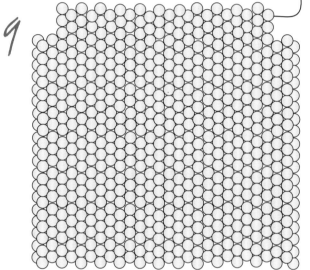

Join flap to opposite side of bottom. Center the flap, fold it over and match up the beads with those on the opposite side of the bag bottom *(Illustration 10)*.
NOTE: You will have 3 high beads making up the unmatched left side and 2 high beads unmatched on the right side.

Take thread through the first high bead on the front, then back through the first high bead on back, etc. The beads will fit together like a zipper. Illustration 11 looks down on the bottom of the bag. The flap beads are gray.

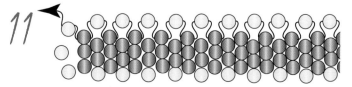

Stitch the open sides closed as shown in Illustrations 12 - 12a.

Now for the lid. The lid is made using the same steps as the body except you begin with more beads. String 60 beads and work as for the body through row 3. Slip the lid over the body of the bag. Is it an easy fit? If the lid is too small to easily slip over the top of the body, make another beginning circle using 64 beads and try again. (Beading is such an exact science!) When the lid fits the body correctly, peyote stitch a total of 15 rows of beads.

Make a flap as you did for the body. If you used 60 beads to begin the lid, the flap should consist of 7 rows of 13 beads each. (If you began with 64 beads, your flap will have 7 rows of 14 beads each.

Stitch the flap to the opposite side of the lid just as you did for the body, but *do not* sew up the sides.

Make the strap. Weave a 70" length of thread up through several rows of the bag. Bring the needle out at the left side. String several inches of beads – enough to make the strap the length you desire.

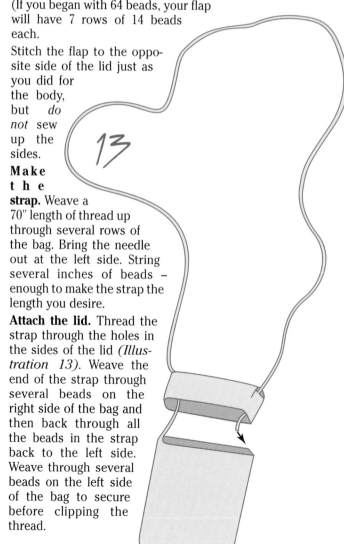

Attach the lid. Thread the strap through the holes in the sides of the lid *(Illustration 13)*. Weave the end of the strap through several beads on the right side of the bag and then back through all the beads in the strap back to the left side. Weave through several beads on the left side of the bag to secure before clipping the thread.

That's It - You're Done!
Doesn't your beadwork look fabulous? Put something special in your new pouch. Wear it in good health!

Create a Darling Beadbag Container

This darling little container works up quickly... you'll want to make one in each color! Use them on your desk to store small items or place in a window and simply enjoy the play of light across the beads. A fringe benefit... These beaded bags are so much fun to play with, you can use them as stress-relief toys.

Cream Beadbag
MATERIALS: Size B beading thread • Size 12 beading needle
Toho Beads:
• 43 grams 6/0 round Sand/Clear #369
• 24 grams 11/0 round transparent luster Light Amber #103

Blue/Purple Beadbag
MATERIALS: Size B beading thread • Size 12 beading needle
Toho Beads:
• 43 grams 6/0 round Purple/Blue #252
• 24 grams 11/0 round transparent Sky Blue #942

Blue/Gray Beadbag
MATERIALS: Size B beading thread • Size 12 beading needle
Toho Beads:
• 43 grams 6/0 round Steel Blue/Crystal AB #288
• 24 grams 11/0 round transparent Smokey Gray #9B

Peyote Stitch - #3

Row 1 - First the bead base. Cut a 36" length of thread. Thread the needle with one end. Thread on three of the larger matte beads. (From now on, we'll just say big beads and little beads.)
Tie the beads into a circle and pass the needle through one of the beads on either side of the knot.

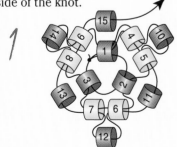

1

Here is how to begin the Beadbag. Note the numbers. The lines show how to thread beads using the peyote stitch - jumping up to catch a bead and then stitching it into the previous row.

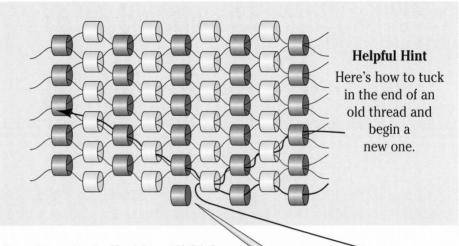

Helpful Hint
Here's how to tuck in the end of an old thread and begin a new one.

Container size is 2" wide x 1¹/₂" high.

Row 2 - Add two beads between each of the three beads forming the circle. Pass the needle up through the first bead of this row. This is called "stepping up". Step up at the end of every row as shown in the illustration.

Row 3 - Add a bead between each of the beads of Row 2.

Row 4 - Add two beads between each of the beads of Row 3.

Rows 5 and 6 - Add a bead between each of the beads of the previous row.

Row 7 - Alternate adding first one, then two beads between each bead of the previous row.

Row 8 - Add a bead between each of the beads of the previous row.

Row 9 - Add one bead between the first two beads of the previous row. Add another bead between the second two beads. Add two beads between the next two. Repeat around the row.

Now we'll bead the sides.

Rows 10 through 24 - Add a bead between the beads of the previous row.

Row 25 - Alternate adding a big bead, then a set of two little beads between the beads of the previous row.

You're through with the big beads. Take a break and have a cup of tea. We'll be working with the little beads to finish the Beadbag.

Row 26 - Add a set of two little beads between each big bead and set of two little beads of the previous row.

Rows 27 through 32 - Add sets of two beads between the sets of previous row.

Row 33 - Alternate adding first one, then two beads between each set of the previous row.

Row 34 - Add a set of two beads between each bead and set of beads of the previous row.

Rows 35 and 36 - Repeat Rows 33 and 34.

Row 37 - Add a single bead between each single bead and set of beads of the previous row.

Continued on page 10

Peyote Beadbag Stitch #3
Continued from page 9

Start beading the bottom of the bag from the center of this diagram. Use the peyote stitch (see diagram on page 9) to jump up a row and catch a new bead, then stitch it back into the previous row. The numbers will help you see how to do this. Beads are shaded dark and light only to help you see the different rows. Smaller circles indicate small beads. The last few rows are not to be spaced out as shown in the diagram, but strung closely together.

Rows 38 through 48 - Add a single bead between each bead of the previous row. Weave thread back down through work for several rows before cutting. See overall chart for the Beadbag below.

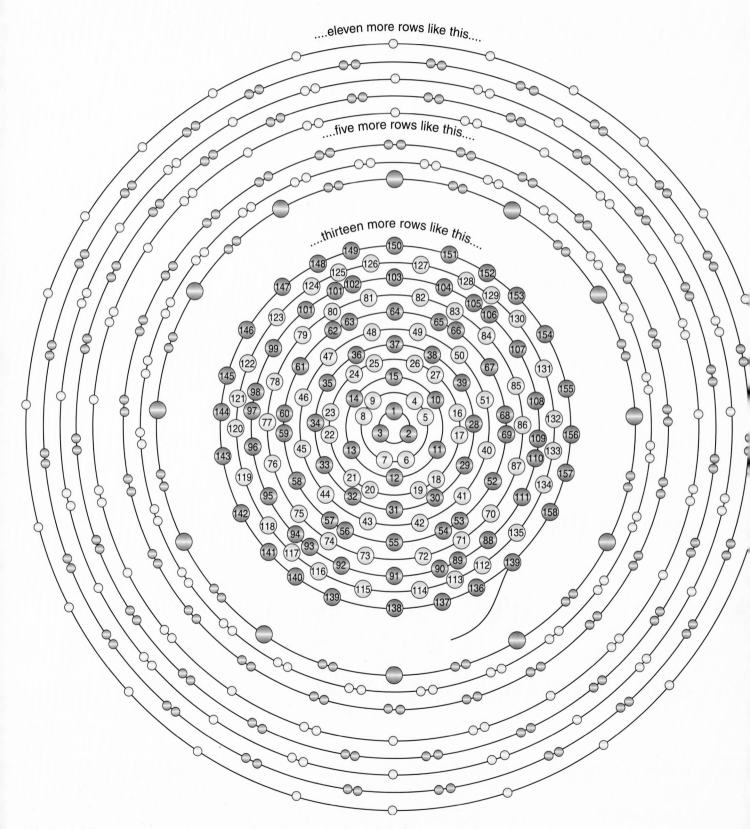

Here's a chart for rows 10 and above

R 10-24	(15 rounds), work even on 24 large beads
R 25	work (1 big, 2 little) around
R 26-32	(7 rounds), work (2 little, 2 little) around
R 33	work (1 little, 2 little) around
R 34	work (2 little, 2 little) around
R 35	work (1 little, 2 little) around
R 36	work (2 little, 2 little) around
R 37-48	(12 rounds), work (1 little bead around

These little beadbag
containers are shown
larger than actual
size for detail.

Never before has a small photo had such a lovely home! Make a photo pouch for yourself, for your favorite mom or grandmother.

Photo Pouch size is 1½" x 2".

Teal/Purple Pouch

MATERIALS: 12 Brass 3mm round beads • 4 Brass ¼" bugle beads • 2 Brass 6mm disk beads • 2 Brass 4mm round beads • ¹⁄₁₆" diameter 1⅜" long styrene tube • Size B beading thread • Size 12 beading needle
Toho Beads:
• 29 grams 11/0 round Metallic Teal/Purple Iris #505

Burgundy Pouch

MATERIALS: 12 Brass 3mm round beads • 4 Brass ¼" bugle beads • 2 Brass 6mm disk beads • 2 Brass 4mm round beads • ¹⁄₁₆" diameter 1⅜" long styrene tube • Size B beading thread • Size 12 beading needle
Toho Beads:
• 29 grams 11/0 round Metallic Burgundy Iris #503

Green Pouch

MATERIALS: 12 Brass 3mm round beads • 4 Brass ¼" bugle beads • 2 Brass 6mm disk beads • 2 Brass 4mm round beads • ¹⁄₁₆" diameter 1⅜" long styrene tube • Size B beading thread • Size 12 beading needle
Toho Beads:
• 29 grams 11/0 round Metallic Emerald Green Iris #451

Peyote Stitch #4

Row 1 - Pour a few seed beads into a small shallow bowl or beading tray. Cut a 48" length of thread. Thread the needle with one end. Thread on 46 seed beads and slide them down to within 6" of the other end.

Pass the needle back through all of the beads again to form a circle *(Illustration 1)*. Bring the needle out just after the first bead strung. The tail won't interfere with the first few stitches!

Row 2 - Thread on a bead, skip the next bead in the row and thread the needle through the second bead *(Illustration 2)*.

Thread on another bead, skip the next bead in the row and thread the beading needle through the second bead *(Illustration 3)*.

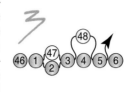

Continue to add beads to the end of the row (23 beads). Notice how the beads from the original circle "share" the space with the new beads? Try to adjust your tension so that the row looks more or less like Illustration 4. To keep the beads from twisting, hold the circle of beads between your thumb and forefinger.

Row 3 - Do you see where your thread has come out of the last bead of Row 2? It's smack dab against the first bead of Row 2. This first bead is called the "step up" bead. You have to "step up" through it to begin the next row *(Illustration 5)*.
You'll begin every row this way. As you can see in Illustration 4, the beads from Row 2 are higher than the rest. In Row 3 we'll place a bead in between each of these higher ones. Thread on a bead and pass your needle through the next high bead *(Illustration 6)*.
Continue adding beads in this manner to the end of the row (23 beads total).

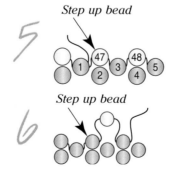

Rows 4 through 9 This is the body of the bag. Step up at the beginning of each row, then add a bead between each of the beads from the previous row. You will be adding 23 beads on every row. Keep your tension consistent throughout.

Here's a hint to help you count the rows: Count on the diagonal as shown in Illustration 7.

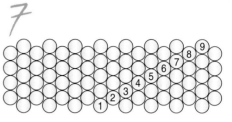

Let's face facts. You're going to run out of thread at some point, but there's no need to panic – or to tie a knot! To end a thread, weave up and down through a few beads on the rows below and clip end.
Weave the new thread up and down through a few beads to come up out of the last bead you added. Weave down to end a thread, weave up to start a new one *(Illustration 8)*.

Weave up to start a new thread.

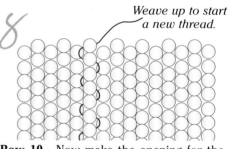

Row 10 - Now make the opening for the photo. Peyote stitch 16 beads.

Row 11 - You are going to turn and work in the opposite direction for this row. Add the first bead of the row as shown in Illustration 9. Work 16 beads total for the row.

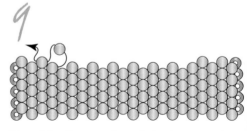

Row 12 - Turn and work in the opposite direction. Add the first bead as shown in Illustration 10. Work 16 beads for the row.

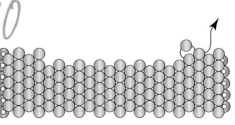

Rows 13 through 36: - Continue to turn and work in the opposite direction for each row. The unworked area is where the photo will go. Now let's get back to working in the round for a few more rows.

Continued on page 14

Complete Row 36 - Instead of turning and working Row 37, string 14 beads and pass the needle through the first bead of the row (*Illustration 11*).

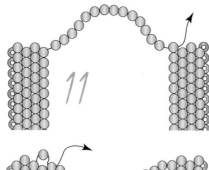

Because you've gone through the first bead of the row, you've just stepped up and you're ready to work Row 37 in the round.

Row 37 - After you've worked the first 16 beads you'll come to the string of 14 beads. Treat them as you did for Row 2, adding a bead between every other one. Illustration 12 shows you how to get started. Illustration 13 shows you how to step up for Row 38.

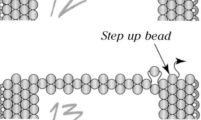

Step up bead

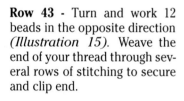

Don't step up.

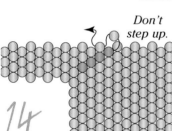

Rows 38 through 41: - Work as for Rows 4 to 9.

Row 42 - After you've added the last bead of Row 41 don't step up. Instead turn and work 12 beads in the opposite direction (*Illustration 14*).

Row 43 - Turn and work 12 beads in the opposite direction (*Illustration 15*). Weave the end of your thread through several rows of stitching to secure and clip end.

OK. The body of the locket is now finished.

Fold it in half so that it matches the illustration on the right and stitch the bottom closed. Folded like this, the beads won't form a zipper. You'll be stitching high beads to high beads along the bottom.

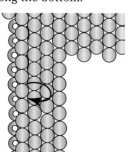

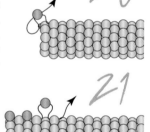

Next, stitch along the sides of the locket as shown at left to make it lay flat.

Next, the tube for the top.

Rows 1 and 2 - String 24 beads. Add another bead (25) and pass your needle back through bead 23 (*Illustration 16*).

Thread on a bead, skip the next bead in the row and thread the needle through the second bead (*Illustration 17*).

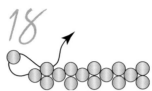

Continue adding beads in this manner to the end of the row. 12 beads total.

Rows 3 through 14 - Thread a bead and pass your needle through the first high bead of the previous row.

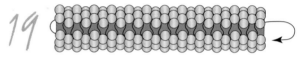

(*Illustration 18*) Add a bead between each of the high beads of the row, 12 beads each row.

Form the tube by folding the rectangle in half. Notice how the high beads fit into each other like a zipper? Stitch the zipper closed as shown in Illustration 19. Stitch through several beads to secure.

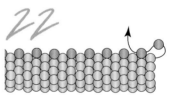

Now we are going to add a small tab to attach the tube to the locket. You'll be adding two rows of peyote stitch on top of the stitches on the tube.

Row 1 - Bring your needle out from a bead on the second row from the end as shown at right. Thread on a bead and slip the needle through the loop of thread that holds the outer beads in place. Pass the needle back through the bead you just added (*Illustration 20*).

Add a bead between each of the high beads on this row (*Illustration 21*).

Row 2 - Turn and work the next row (*Illustration 22*).

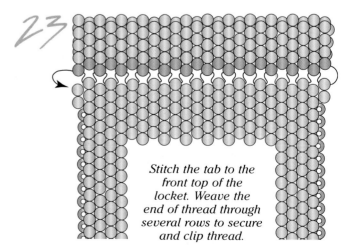

Stitch the tab to the front top of the locket. Weave the end of thread through several rows to secure and clip thread.

Let's add the front flap. You are going to add another row of stitching to the tube just in front of the tab. The beginning is done just a little differently. Follow the illustrations and you shouldn't have any trouble.

Row 1 - Bring your needle in through the first bead of a row. Thread a bead and take the needle through the next bead of the row. *(Illustration 24)*

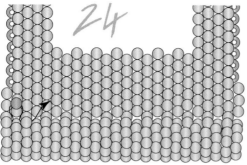

Continue to add beads to the end of the row. **Rows 2 through 20** - Turn and begin working the next row. *(Illustration 25)*

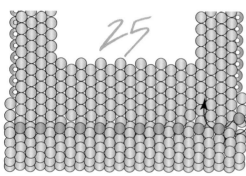

Row 21 - Decrease at the beginning of the row. *(Illustration 26)*

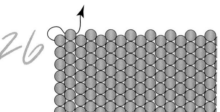

Row 22 - Decrease at the beginning of the row. *(Illustration 27)*

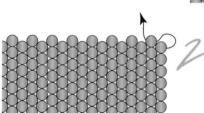

Rows 23 through 35 - Work in flat peyote - 9 beads per row. *(Illustration 28)*

Rows 36 through 44 - Decrease at the beginning of each row. *(Illustration 28)*

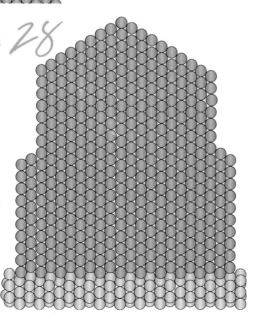
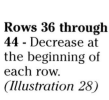

You're almost there!

Follow the beading diagram in Illustration 29 to make the strap. Try using doubled thread to make the strap stronger.

Slip the plastic tube into the bead tube. Add the disk and seed bead end-caps as shown. Tie the loose ends of thread in a knot to secure bead.

That's it - You're Done!

Now, find your most precious photo, trim it to the right size and slip it inside your new locket – perfect!

Bead an elegant Peyote Scroll Frame! You'll have great fun showing off that special photo.

Scroll size is 1¹/₂" x 1³/₄".

Teal/Purple Scroll

MATERIALS: 8 Brass 3mm bicone beads • 6 Brass 3mm round beads • 6 Brass 6mm disk beads • 2 Brass 4mm round beads• ¹/₈" diameter 1⁵/₈" long styrene tube • Size B beading thread • Size 12 beading needle
Toho Treasure Beads:
• 12 grams Metallic Teal/Purple Iris #505

Burgundy Scroll

MATERIALS: 8 Brass 3mm bicone beads • 6 Brass 3mm round beads • 6 Brass 6mm disk beads • 2 Brass 4mm round beads • Two ¹/₈" diameter 1⁵/₈" long styrene tube • Size B beading thread • Size 12 beading needle
Toho Treasure Beads:
• 12 grams Metallic Burgundy Iris #503

Green Scroll

MATERIALS: 8 Brass 3mm bicone beads • 6 Brass 3mm round beads • 6 Brass 6mm disk beads • 2 Brass 4mm round beads • ¹/₈" diameter 1⁵/₈" long styrene tube • Size B beading thread • Size 12 beading needle
Toho Treasure Beads:
• 12 grams Metallic Emerald Green Iris #507

Peyote Stitch #5

Rows 1 and 2 - First we'll bead two flat pieces which will later be used to cover the brass tubes.

Thread a needle with 48" of thread, leave an 8" tail and string 32 beads. Add another bead (33) and pass your needle back through bead 31 as shown in Illustration 1.

Thread on a bead, skip the next bead in the row and thread the needle through second bead (*Illustration 2*).

Thread on another bead, skip the next bead in the row and thread the needle through the second bead (*Illustration 3*).

Notice how the beads from the first row "share" the space with the new beads? Try to adjust your tension so that the row looks more or less like Illustration 4. Continue adding beads in this fashion to the end of the row, 16 beads total.

Row 3 - Thread a bead and pass your needle through the first high bead of the previous row (*Illustration 5*). Add a bead between each of the high beads of the row, 16 beads total (*Illustration 6*).

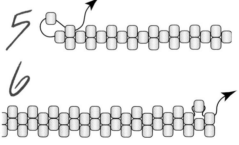

Rows 4 through 18 - Continue to add beads between each of the high beads of the previous row.
Helpful Hint: To help you count the rows, count on the diagonal as shown in Illustration 7.

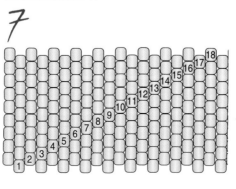

Let's face facts. You're going to run out of thread at some point, but there's no need to panic – or to tie a knot! To end a thread, weave up and down through a few beads on the rows below. Clip thread end. Cut a 36" length of thread and weave up and down through a few beads to come up out of the last bead you added. Weave down to end a thread, weave up to start a new one (*Illustration 8*).

Weave up to start a new thread.

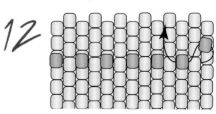

Now add the back panel. Weave down through a few edge beads as shown in Illustration 9. Bring your needle in through the first bead of a row as shown.

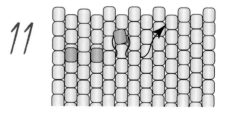

Thread on a bead and take needle through the next bead of the row (*Illustration 10*).

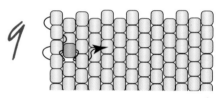

Continue to add beads to the end of the row (*Illustration 11*).

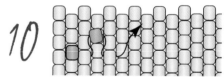

Turn and begin working next row (*Illustration 12*).

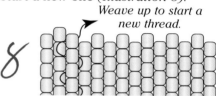

Continued on page 18

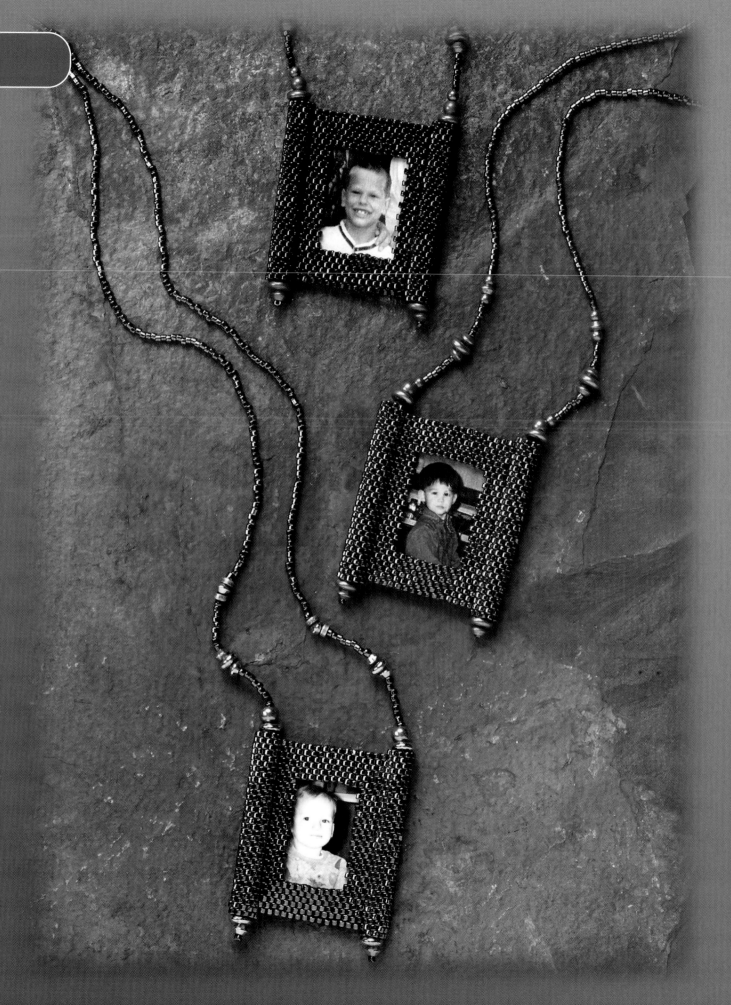

Peyote Scroll Stitch #5
Continued from page 16

Continue for a total of 16 rows. Refer to Illustrations 13 and 14 to help you remember how to start new rows. Illustration 15 is a tiny picture of how the piece should look when it's completed.

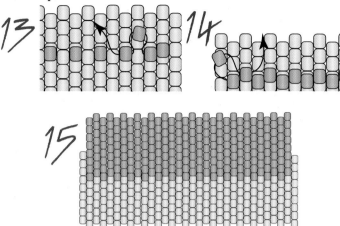

Make another section directly in front of the one you've just completed. Begin in the same manner as before and work 6 rows *(Illustrations 16 -17)*.

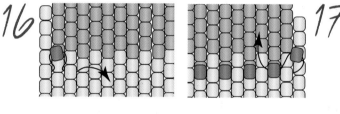

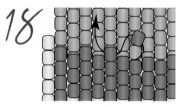

Work the first three beads of the seventh row, turn and work three beads in the opposite direction *(Illustration 18)*.
Continue for a total of 10 three-bead rows.

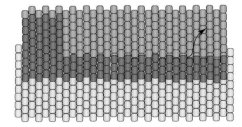

Weave thread back through row 6 and exit as shown *(Illustration 19)*.

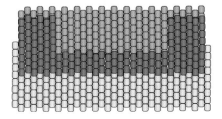

Work 10 three-bead rows on this side. Your piece should look like Illustration 20.

Have you had fun so far?
I hope so, because you get to do it all again for the other half! That's right – go back to step 1 and repeat everything up to this point. Don't worry, we'll wait for you.

OK! That wasn't so bad was it?
You've completed all the pieces. Now for the fun part – putting it all together! We'll begin with the back seam. Line up your two halves as shown in Illustration 21 and match them up like a zipper. (Isn't it neat the way it does that?) Now just stitch them together.

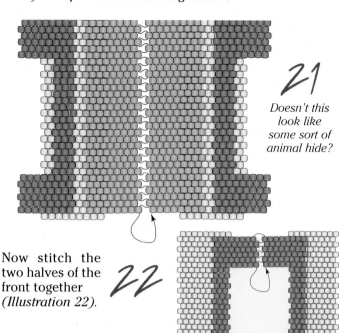

Doesn't this look like some sort of animal hide?

Now stitch the two halves of the front together *(Illustration 22)*.

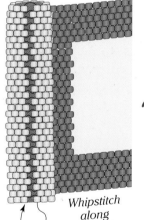

Whipstitch along bottom edge.

Next, enclose the brass tubes b "zipping up" the sides. It may be bit of a tight fit *(Illustration 23)*.

Whipstitch the bottom edges of th front and back pieces together, too

There's only one thing left, the strap. Follow Illustration 24 to make the strap. Use doubled thread to make the strap stronger. Tie the loose ends together and...

That's It – You're Done!
Doesn't your beadwork look terrific? Put a photo of someone special in your new frame.

You'll Love Making a Sea Spray Bottle with Stopper

designed by Mary Harrison & Donetta Driscoll

Branch fringe hangs from the stopper and the base of this tiny beaded bottle. Add a simple chain and you can wear this delicate beauty with a sense of accomplishment and pride. The pearly cream color will complement any outfit and your friends will surely want to know where you found such a dramatic piece of jewelry!

Sea Spray Bottle size is 3" with fringe.

Buttermilk Bottle

MATERIALS: 1" test tube bottle with cork stopper • Size B beading thread • Size 12 beading needle • White glue • Clear nail polish

Toho Beads:
• 12 grams 15/0 round lustered Buttermilk #122
• 2 grams 15/0 round lustered Baby Pink #126
• 2 grams 15/0 round lustered Rose #127

Peyote Stitch #6

Row 1 - Pour a few Buttermilk seed beads into a small shallow bowl or beading tray. Cut a 48" length of thread. Thread the needle with one end. Thread 24 seed beads and slide them down to within 6" of the other end. Pass the needle back through all of the beads again to form a circle *(Illustration 1)*. Bring the needle out just after the first bead strung. This way the tail won't interfere with first few stitches!

Row 2 - Slip the ring of beads over the neck of the bottle. Thread on a bead, skip the next bead in the row and thread the needle through the second bead *(Illustration 2)*. Continue to add a bead between every other bead to the end of the row, 12 beads total *(Illustration 3)*. Notice how the beads from the original circle "share" the space with the new beads? Try to adjust your tension so that the row looks more or less like Illustration 4.

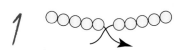

Row 3 - Do you see where your thread has come out of the last bead of Row 2? It's smack dab against the first bead of Row 2. This first bead is called the "step up" bead. You have to "step up" through it to begin the next row *(Illustration 5)*. You'll begin every row

this way. As you can see in Illustration 4, the beads from Row 2 are higher than the rest. In Row 3 we'll place a bead in between each of these higher ones. Thread on a bead and pass your needle through the next high bead *(Illustration 6)*. Continue adding beads in this manner to the end of the row, 12 beads total.

Step up bead

Step up bead

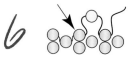

Rows 4 through 16 - Step up at the beginning of each row, then add a bead between each of the beads from the previous row. You will be adding 12 beads on every row. Keep your tension consistent throughout.

Thirty rows *should* cover the bottle. However, every bottle is a little different. It may only take you 27 rows - then again, it may take 35! The number of rows isn't important. Remember, this is a stress free zone!

Helpful Hint - After you've completed a few rows of peyote stitching, smear a little bit of white glue near the top edge of the bottle, then slide your beadwork up to the edge. When the glue dries, it will hold your ring of beads in place as you stitch the rest of the bottle.

Let's face facts: You're going to run out of thread at some point, but there's no need to panic – or to tie a knot! To end a thread, weave up and down through a few beads on the rows below and clip the end. Weave the new thread up and down through a few beads to come up out of the last bead you added. Weave down to end a thread, weave up to start a new one *(Illustration 7)*.

Weave up to start a new thread.

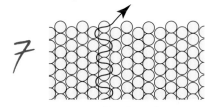

Continued on page 20

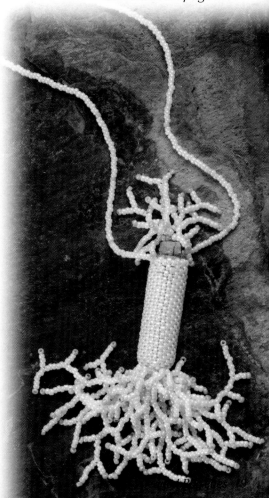

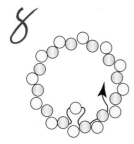

Let's stitch the bottom of the bottle. Illustration 8 is the view from the bottom of the bottle looking up. **Row 31:** Step up to begin the row. Add a bead between the first two high beads, make the next stitch without a bead. Continue in this manner around the bottom of the bottle. You'll add six beads total.

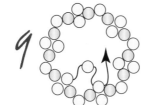

Row 32 - Step up though the first bead of Row 31. Add a bead between each of the 6 beads of Row 31.

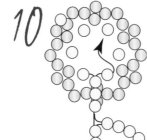

Row 33 - Inside Fringe Row: Step up to begin row. Place a strand of fringe between each of the beads in Row 32. You will add 6 strands of fringe for this row (*Illustration 10*).

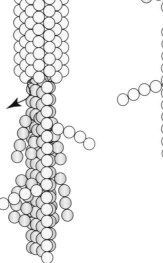

Outside Row - Weave your needle back to the last 12 bead row of the bottle. Add 12 strands for the row (*Illustration 11*).

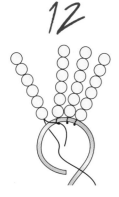

Add fringe to the stopper. Leaving a long tail of thread, make a strand of branch fringe just like the fringe for the bottle but begin with 8 to 14 beads. Tie a knot with the tail and the bead strand around the eye hook on top of the cork stopper. Make six strands of fringe and tie each in place with the tail thread. Dot knots with clear nail polish. Clip tail thread close (*Illustration 12*).

Add the Strap. After weaving through several rows to secure, bring needle out at the top left of the bottle.

Beading Pattern. *Thread on 12 Buttermilk beads, 2 Baby Pink, 1 Rose, and 2 Baby Pink. Repeat from * two more times. Thread Buttermilk beads for the longest part of the strap and then reverse the beading pattern for the right side of the strap. Enter at the right side of bottle. Weave through a few stitches and thread needle back through all beads in strap to the left side of bottle. Weave through several rows of stitching. Clip thread close.

How to Make Branch Fringe:

Thread on 30 Buttermilk beads, 3 Baby Pink and a Rose bead. Skip the Rose bead and pass the needle back through the Baby Pink beads and 5 Buttermilk beads. *Thread on 3 Baby Pink beads and 1 Rose bead. Pass the needle back through the 3 Baby Pink beads and up through 5 more Buttermilk beads. Repeat from * to the end of the strand.

HELPFUL HINT - Vary the numbers of beads in the beginning strand and on the branches to add variety and interest.

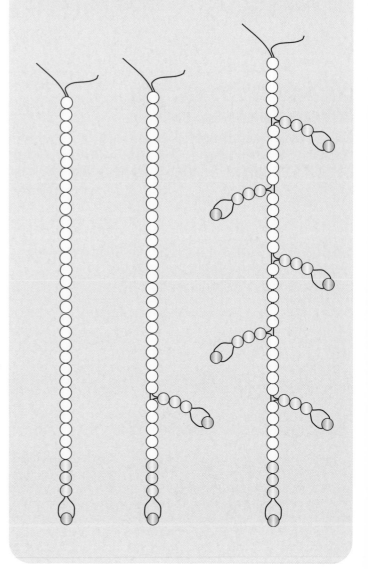

You're Finished!
What will you put in your bottle? Your favorite oil? Fairie dust? A wish?

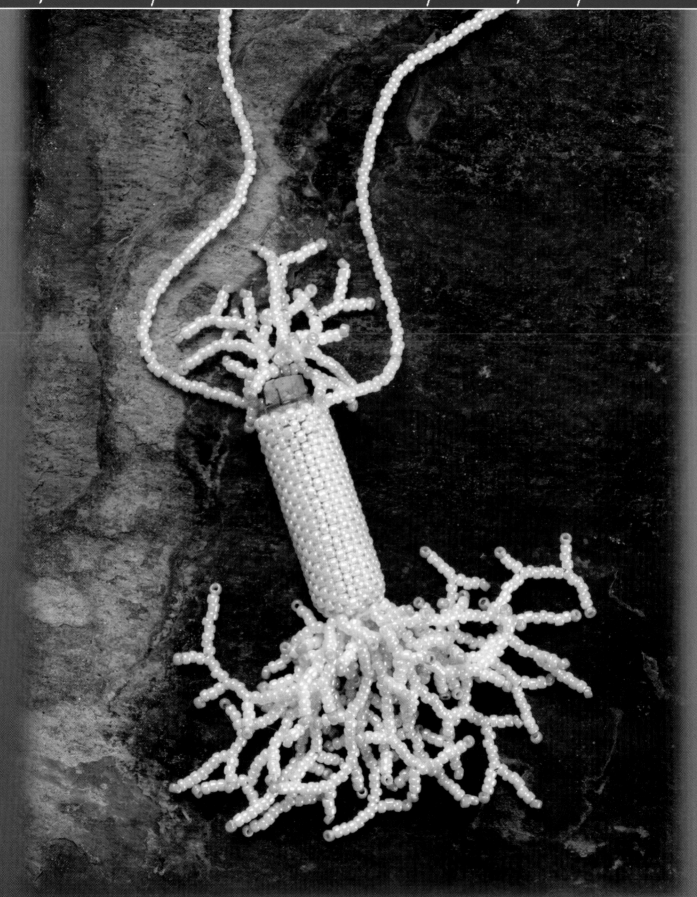

A Beautiful Garden Trellis Bottle Necklace

The dainty Garden Trellis Bottle is a perfect place to keep your tiniest treasures. Learn the basics of the net stitch and how to make a variation of branch fringe as you complete this lovely piece. The colors bring to mind the azure skies and puffy white clouds of a perfect spring day!

designed by Mary Harrison
& Donetta Driscoll

Trellis Bottle size is 3" with fringe.

Cobalt Bottle

MATERIALS: 1" bottle (mason jar) with cork stopper • Size B beading thread • Size 12 beading needle • Clear fingernail polish

Toho Beads:
• 4 grams 15/0 hex Silver lined Cobalt #28
• 12 grams 15/0 hex Silver lined Crystal #21
• 2 grams 15/0 hex Silver lined Light Blue #33

Net Stitch

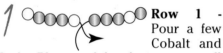 **Row 1 -** Pour a few Cobalt and Light Blue seed beads into a small shallow bowl or beading tray. Cut a 48" length of thread. Thread the needle with one end. Thread seven groups of one Light Blue and three Cobalt beads for a total of 28 beads. Pass the needle back through all of the beads again to form a circle (*Illustration 1*). Slip the circle around the neck of the bottle and tighten.

Bring the needle out just after the first bead strung. This way the tail won't interfere with the first few stitches!

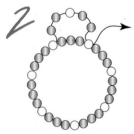 **Row 2 -** Make sure your thread is coming out of a Light Blue bead. Thread on 2 Cobalt, a Light Blue and 2 Cobalt beads. If you have never done net stitch before or if these beads are just a little small for you, it's a good idea to make the center bead a different color. Pass the needle through the next Light Blue bead in the ring (*Illustration 2*). Thread 2 Cobalt, a Light Blue and 2 Cobalt beads and pass the needle through the next Light Blue bead in the ring. Continue until you have added seven groups of beads around the ring.

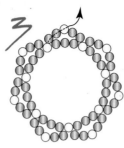 **Row 3 -** When you reach the end of the row, you'll have to "step up" to begin the next row by passing the needle through three beads of the first group and emerging from the center Light Blue bead of the group (*Illustration 3*).

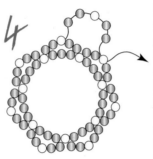 **Rows 4 through 10 -** Work as for Row 3, stepping up at the beginning of each row and adding seven groups of 5 beads around the bottle. Ten rows should be enough to reach the bottom edge of the bottle, but every bottle is a bit different. It may only take nine rows to reach the bottom edge, then again, it may take 11 or 12! The number of rows isn't important. Remember - this is a stress free zone.

 **Bottom of Bottle -** We are going to decrease the size of each group in order to pull the net in under the bottle. Begin the row by stepping up through three beads and emerging from the center point (Light Blue bead) of a group. Thread a Cobalt, a Light Blue and a Cobalt in each group around. As you tighten each group you will notice the net pulling in toward the center bottom of the bottle. Illustrations 5 and 6 show the view looking up from the bottom of the bottle.

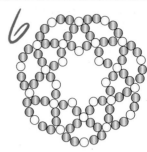 **Let's face facts.** You're going to run out of thread at some point, but there's no need to panic – or to tie a knot!

To end a thread, weave up and down through a few beads on the rows below and clip the end. Weave the new thread up and down through a few beads to come up out of the last bead you added. Weave down to end a thread, weave up to start a new one (*Illustration 7*).

Weave up to start a new thread.

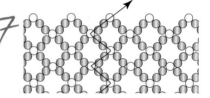

Are You Ready to Make Some Fringe? The fringe is the best part of this project! Follow these beading diagram to make branch fringe.

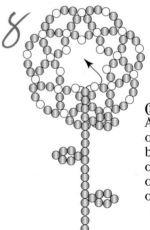 **Row 1 (inside row) -** Add a strand of bead fringe between each of the points of the previous row (*Illustration 8*).

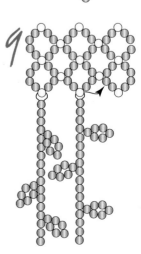 **Row 2 (outside row) -** Weave your needle to the row on the bottom outside edge of the bottle. Add a strand of fringe to each of the center beads of the row (*Illustration 9*).

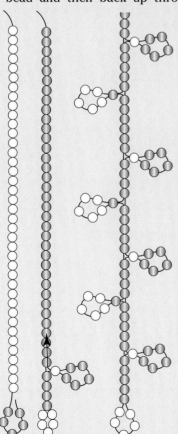

10 **Add fringe to the stopper.** Leaving a long tail of thread, make a strand of branch fringe just like the fringe for the bottle but begin with only 8 to 14 beads. Tie a knot with the tail and the bead strand around the eye hook on top of the cork stopper. Make five more strands of fringe in the same manner, knotting each strand of fringe with the tail thread. Dot the 4 knots with clear nail polish. Clip the tail thread close.

Add the strap. After weaving through several rows to secure, bring needle out at the top left of the bottle.
Beading pattern:
*Thread on 12 Cobalt beads, 2 Crystal, 1 Light Blue, and 2 Crystal. Repeat from * two more times.
Thread Cobalt beads for the rest of the strap, then reverse the beading pattern for the other side. Enter at the right side of bottle. Weave through a few stitches and thread needle back through all beads in the strap to the left side of bottle. Weave through several rows of stitching. Clip thread close.

What will you put in your bottle? Sand from your favorite beach? Scented oil? A love note?

How to Make Branch Fringe:

Thread on 25 Cobalt beads, a Crystal bead and 5 Light Blue beads. Thread needle back up through the Crystal bead. Pass the needle up through five Cobalt beads and thread on a Light Blue bead and five Crystal beads. Pass needle back through the Light Blue bead and then back up through five more Cobalt beads on the strand. Alternate adding Crystal and Light Blue "leaves". Repeat the process to the top of the strand. On the next strand of fringe you'll string 25 Cobalt, a Light Blue and 5 Crystal, then come up through the Light Blue bead. Come back up through five Cobalt beads. Thread on one Crystal and five Light Blue beads. Go back through the Crystal bead. Alternate adding Crystal and Light Blue "leaves" to the top of the strand. NOTE: This is just a template. You can vary the number of beads in each strand of fringe as well as the number of beads between the "leaves".

Add a touch of elegance to this tiny beaded bag with a crystal point closure. How eye-catching and beautiful!

Crystal Bag size is 1¹/₂" wide x 1³/₄" high.

Gold Bag

MATERIALS: 12 Brass 3mm bicone beads • 6 Brass 6mm disk beads • Wire wrapped crystal point • Size B beading thread • Size 12 beading needle

Toho Beads:
• 30 grams 11/0 round matte galvanized Gold #557F

Taupe Bag

MATERIALS: 12 Brass 3mm bicone beads • 6 Brass 6mm disk beads • Wire wrapped crystal point • Size B beading thread • Size 12 beading needle

Toho Beads:
• 30 grams 11/0 round matte galvanized Dark Taupe #564F

Kiwi Bag

MATERIALS:12 Brass 3mm bicone beads • 6 Brass 6mm disk beads • Wire wrapped crystal point • Size B beading thread • Size 12 beading needle

Toho Beads:
• 30 grams 11/0 round matte galvanized Kiwi #560F

Let's talk about some terms.

A **"group"** is the number of beads added with each stitch.

A **"round"** is a series of groups joined at the end to create a tube for body of bag.

A **"row"** is a series of groups **that are worked** then turned and worked back the other way for flap.

Let's bead.

Cut a 48" length of thread. Thread the needle on one end. Thread on six beads. Slide them down the thread, leaving the last 12" of thread free. Wrap this end around the index finger of your free hand. You'll pull against this as you tighten the first few stitches.

Brick Stitch #1

Round 1 - Now thread the needle back through all six beads. Adjust work into two groups of three beads each (Illustrations 1 - 2).

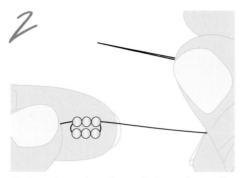

String three beads and thread needle back through second group of three beads and the new beads. Now you have three groups of three beads each (Illustration 3).

Continue until you have 32 groups. Join the first group to the last by running needle through both groups a couple of times, ending with thread coming out from top of round (Illustration 4).

Now that you've begun the tube for the bottom of the purse, place tube over your index finger and brace the work against it as you bead.

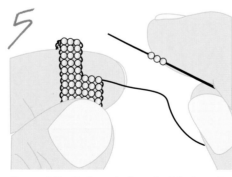

Round 2 - String six beads. Notice the loops connecting each group of beads across the top edge of Round 1. Skip the loop just next to the thread and hook the needle under the second loop. Bring needle back up through last three beads (Illustration 6).

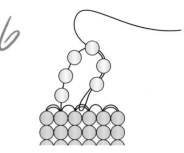

String three beads, hook needle under next loop & bring needle back up through beads (Illustration 7).

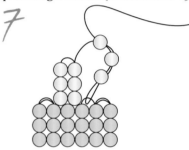

Continue to make another round with 32 groups of 3 beads. Join the ends of the round by threading needle down through the top of the first group and up through the last group (Illustration 8).

Pass needle back down through the top of the first group and up through the second group to stabilize them (Illustration 8a).

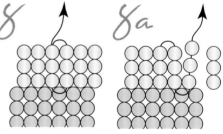

Rounds 3 through 9 - Work as for Round 2 to complete the tube for the bottom of the purse.

Let's face facts – You're going to run out of thread at some point, but there's no need to panic – or to tie a knot! To end a thread, weave up and down through a couple of bead groups on 2 or 3 rounds below.

Clip thread end. Cut a 36" length of thread and weave up and down through a couple of bead groups on 2 or 3 rounds to come up out of the last group of beads you added. Weave down to end a thread, weave up to start a new one (Illustration 9).

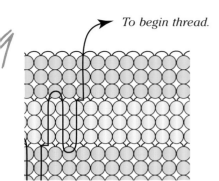

To begin thread.

Now take a break and drink a cup of tea! Beads were found in an ancient burial site in France. Archeologists have estimated the date as 38,000 B.C. From these primitive beginnings to elegant Venetian glass beads and precious metals, beads continue to fascinate, entertain and adorn humans.

Now let's work in rows!

Row 10 (begin flap) - Work 16 groups with 2 beads instead of 3 in each group. Work the first two groups in second loop.

Row 11 - Turn purse over to begin round. Thread 4 beads. Continue across. You have 15 groups with 2 beads in each group.

Row 12 - Work as for Round 11 to make 14 groups of 2 beads.

Rows 13 through 15 - Turn bag over. Thread 6 beads at the beginning of each row. Make 3 bead groups across each row. Turn at end of each row. There should be 11 groups on Row 15.

Row 16 (flap opening) - Turn purse over. Work 4 groups of 3 beads. Bring needle back down through the top of the third group. Weave thread through groups of Row 15, eventually bringing needle back up at fourth loop from the end of that row. String six beads and work next two groups, beginning in fourth loop from end as illustrated. Work last 2 groups *(Illustration 10)*.

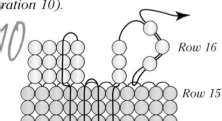

Row 16

Row 15

Row 17 (to end flap opening) - Turn bag over. Pass needle down through next to last group of 3 beads on Row 16, then weave through 2 groups on Row 15. Come back up through the same group you went down through *(Illustration 11)*.

Continued on page 26

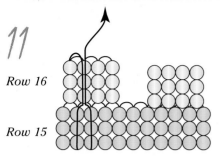

Row 16

Row 15

Thread 6 beads to work first two groups as before. Add 3 beads for next group as you did for Round 1 of bag *(Illustration 12)*.

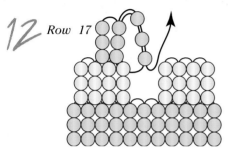

Row 17

Add 3 groups as you did in Round 1. Work a group in each of the next 2 loops.

Row 18 - Turn purse over. Begin this row as you did Row 17, thread 4 beads and make four 2-bead groups across the row.

Row 19 - Turn purse over, thread 2 beads. Make three 1-bead groups across the row.

Row 20 - Turn purse over, thread 2 beads. Make two 1 bead groups across the row.

Row 21 - Thread one bead. To secure thread, weave down through several rows of flap, then weave back up through a few rows.

Clip thread end close *(Illustration 13. See Illustration 14.)*

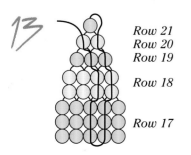

Row 21
Row 20
Row 19

Row 18

Row 17

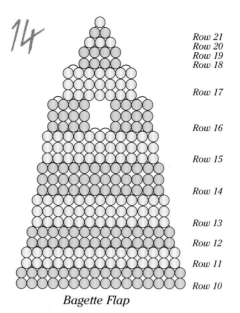

Row 21
Row 20
Row 19
Row 18

Row 17

Row 16

Row 15

Row 14

Row 13

Row 12

Row 11

Row 10

Bagette Flap

Closure loop - Flatten body of purse and fold flap over. Note the bead groups on purse front just to the right and left side of flap opening. These should be the center 4 groups on Round 6.

Thread needle with 36" of thread and weave up and down through several bead groups on purse front to secure thread end. Bring needle up through the bottom 2 beads only of the appropriate group (the sixth group from one side) on purse front. *(Illustration 15)*

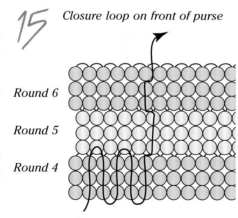

Closure loop on front of purse

Round 6

Round 5

Round 4

Thread 4 beads. Add groups of 2 beads as you did in Round 1. Work enough groups to accommodate your crystal point easily. This will be 8 groups, more or less. Fold the flap over the loop, pull the loop through the opening in the flap and check to see if your crystal fits in the loop. Skip 2 groups across the purse front from where you began the loop. Join the end of the loop through the bottom 2 beads of the next group on the same round of purse front. Weave the thread to secure it, clip end close.

Bag's done. Now let's make the strap. Cut 70" of thread. Using doubled thread, weave through several bead groups on several rows on back of purse, eventually bringing needle up through the group at top side of purse just in front of the flap. String beads for strap following the beading diagram, then add seed beads for 19 or 20". Turn the beading diagram upside down to bead other end of strap in a mirror image of first side.

Bring needle down through top of bead group on Round 9 at opposite side of purse just in front of flap. Do not cut thread.

OK. Next, the keeper for the crystal. Weave needle down through a bead group on Round 8, then weave back up through the bead group right next to it *(Illustration 17)*. If possible, bring needle out through the same group on Round 9 where you attached the strap. Things may be tight. If so, bring needle up through group just next to that group.

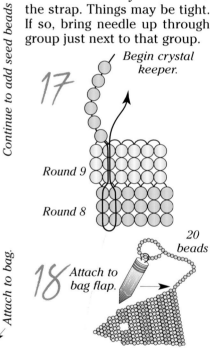

Begin crystal keeper.

Round 9

Round 8

20 beads

Attach to bag flap.

Continue to add seed beads for 19" to 20".

Attach to bag.

String 35 seed beads for keeper. Thread hanging loop of crystal point over these beads and thread needle back through the first 20 beads strung to form a loop at the end of the keeper. Bring needle back down through the same bead group where you began the keeper. Weave up and down through several groups on purse front. Clip thread close. Fold flap opening over closure loop, insert crystal point through loop and hold bottom of purse flat. Use the 12" of thread that you left free at the beginning of the purse to whipstitch loops across bottom of Round 1 together to close purse bottom.

Create a Beautiful Bag-ette Purse Necklace

Here's a real brick stitch sampler! Enjoy learning the brick stitch while making a pretty amulet bag using several sizes and shapes of beads in metallic and earth tone colors.

Bag-ette Purse size is 1½" wide x 1¾" high.

Bronze Bag-ette
MATERIALS: 4 Brass 3mm bicone beads • 2 Brass 4mm cube beads • .006 Power Pro braided beading thread • Size 12 beading needle
Toho Beads:
• 4 grams 6/0 round Bronze Bronze #221
• 4 grams 6/0 round matte Soft Brown #702
• 9 grams 11/0 round Bronze Bronze #221
• 6 grams 3 bugle Bronze Bronze #221
• 6 grams 3 bugle matte Soft Brown #702
• 4 grams 11/0 round matte Soft Brown #702

Copper Bag-ette
MATERIALS: 4 Brass 3mm bicone beads • 2 Brass 4mm cube beads • .006 Power Pro braided beading thread • Size 12 beading needle
Toho Beads:
• 4 grams 6/0 round Bronze Copper #222
• 4 grams 6/0 round matte Cabernet #703
• 9 grams 11/0 round Bronze Copper #222
• 4 grams 11/0 round matte Cabernet #703
• 6 grams 3 bugle Bronze Copper #222
• 6 grams 3 bugle matte Cabernet #703

Brick Stitch #2

NOTE: Bugle beads are basically glass tubes which may over time cut the thread on which they are strung. Use care when choosing bugles for this project. Do not use beads with broken or sharp edges.

Let's bead. Cut a 48" length of thread. Thread the needle with one end. Slide on two bugle beads. Slide them down the thread, leaving the last 12" of thread free. Wrap this end around the index finger of your free hand. You'll pull against this as you tighten the first few stitches.

Row 1 - Thread the needle back through both beads. Adjust your work as shown in Illustration 1.

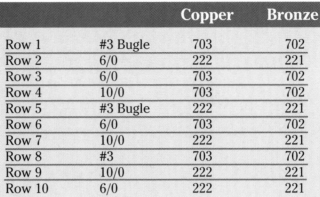

		Copper	Bronze
Row 1	#3 Bugle	703	702
Row 2	6/0	222	221
Row 3	6/0	703	702
Row 4	10/0	703	702
Row 5	#3 Bugle	222	221
Row 6	6/0	703	702
Row 7	10/0	222	221
Row 8	#3	703	702
Row 9	10/0	222	221
Row 10	6/0	222	221

String another bugle bead. Thread needle back through second bugle and the new bugle. Now you have three bugles in a row *(Illustration 2)*. Continue until you have 40 bugles.

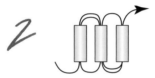

Join the first bugle to the last by running needle through both beads a couple of times, ending with thread coming out from top of row *(Illustration 3)*.

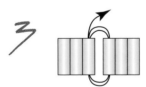

Place this tube of bugle beads over your index finger and brace the beads against it as you work around.

Row 2 - String two big seed beads. Notice the loops connecting the bugle beads across the top edge of Row 1. Skip the first two loops just next to the thread and hook the needle under the third loop. Bring needle back up through the last big seed bead *(Illustration 4)*.

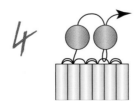

Thread another big seed bead. Hook needle under second loop from last stitch and bring needle back up through the same bead.

(Illustration 5)

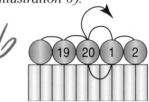

Finish the row.
Join the ends of the row by threading the needle down through the top of the first big bead and up through the 20th (last bead) *(Illustration 6)*.

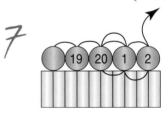

Pass needle down through the top of the first bead and up through the second to stabilize them *(Illustration 7)*.

Continued on page 28

Row 3 - String two big seed beads. Skip the first loop just next to the thread and hook the needle under the second loop. Bring needle back up through the last big seed bead *(Illustration 8)*.

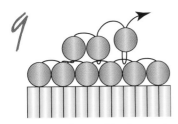

String another big seed bead, hook needle under the next loop and bring needle back up through the same bead *(Illustration 9)*.

Continue to make another row of 20 large glass beads. Join the ends and stabilize the first two beads as in Row 2 *(Illustrations 6 - 7)*.

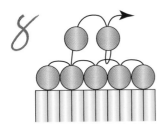

Let's face facts. You're going to run out of thread at some point, but there's no need to panic – or to tie a knot! To end a thread, weave up and down through a few beads on the rows below. Clip thread end. Cut a 36" length of thread and weave up and down through a few beads to come up out of the last group of beads you added. Weave down to end a thread, weave up to start a new one *(Illustration 10)*.

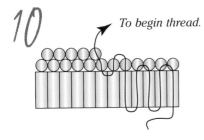

To begin thread.

Double the Fun!
Row 4 - Thread four small seed beads on needle. Pass needle through the first loop and back up through the last two beads *(Illustration 11)*.

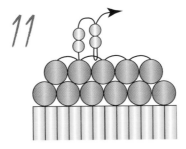

Arrange into two groups of two beads each. Thread two more beads on needle, pass needle through next loop and back up through the last two beads *(Illustration 12)*.

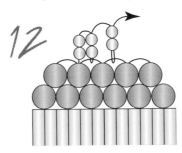

String two more beads and thread the needle back under the SAME loop you worked the last group *(Illustration 13)*. Continue to work two groups of two beads in every loop around. Join the last group to the first group and stabilize the first stitch *(Illustrations 6 - 7)*. Treat each group of two beads as a single unit.

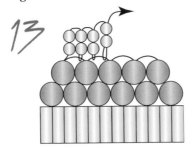

By now you have probably noticed a pattern. Seed beads, bugles and little brass beads are approximately the same diameter - there are 40 beads in each row. The larger seed beads are twice the diameter of the smaller beads. There are 20 beads in these rows.

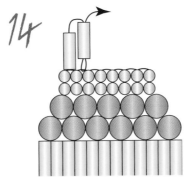

Row 5 - Thread on two bugle beads. Hook the needle through the second loop and then back through the last bugle *(Illustration 14)*.
Thread another bugle and work a stitch in the next loop *(Illustration 15)*.

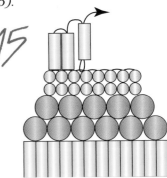

Work a total of 40 bugle beads in the row. Join the ends and stabilize.

Row 6 - Work as for Row 2 *(Illustration 16)*.

Row 7 - Work the row in brass beads, two stitches in every loop around. You should end up with 40 brass beads in the row *(Illustration 17)*.

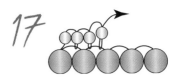

Row 8 - Work the row in bugle beads *(Illustration 18)*.

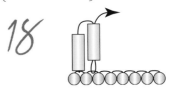

Row 9 - Work the row in small seed beads *(Illustration 19)*.

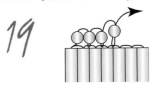

Row 10 - Work the row in big seed beads *(Illustration 20)*.

[af]ter completing Row 10, weave the
[th]read through several stitches and clip
[it] close.

[M]ake the Strap. - Cut 70" of
[th]read. Using doubled
[th]read, weave through sever-
[al] beads eventually bringing
[ne]edle out through a bugle
[be]ad on the first (top) row.
[St]ring beads for strap using
[yo]ur remaining beads and
[re]ferring to Illustration 21.
[Th]en add seed beads for 20".
[T]urn the beading diagram
[up]side down to bead a mir-
[ro]r image of the first side.

[B]ring needle down through a
[bu]gle on the opposite side.
[W]eave thread through a few
[be]ads on side and come
[ba]ck out up through the
[bu]gle next to the entry bead
[(I]llustration 22).

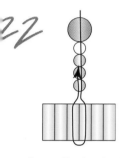

[T]hread needle back through
[al]l beads on strap. Bring nee-
[dl]e back into the purse
[th]rough a bead next to the
[en]try bugle.
[Fi]nishing - Whipstitch the
[bo]ttom loops to close.

Open the little

bag-ette purse and

[p]ut something in it —

a tiny sand dollar?

Pebbles from

the beach?

It's up to you!

21

*Continue
to add
seed beads
for 20".*

Bead a unique Triangle Tote. Worked with two or three beads at a time, the brick stitch works up fast so you can complete this futuristic accessory in no time at all!

Triangle Tote size is 2" x 2¹/₂".

Bronze Tote
MATERIALS: 2 Black glass 6mm disk beads • Size B beading thread • Size 12 beading needle
Toho Beads:
• 23 grams 11/0 round matte Black #610
• 8 grams 11/0 round Bronze Bronze #221

Hematite Tote
MATERIALS: 2 Black glass 6mm disk beads • Size B beading thread • Size 12 beading needle
Toho Beads:
• 23 grams 11/0 round matte Black #610
• 8 grams 11/0 round Metallic Hematite #81

Copper Tote
MATERIALS: 2 Black glass 6mm disk beads • Size B beading thread • Size 12 beading needle
Toho Beads:
• 23 grams 11/0 round matte Black #610
• 8 grams 11/0 round Bronze Copper #222

The Big Picture

Sometimes it helps to get an overview of the entire process before you begin a new project. So when you ask yourself "Why am I doing this?" you will be able to give yourself the correct answer! You are going to be making the body of the bag in two pieces – a Black diamond and a metallic triangle. Next we'll make a beaded circle, work a diamond on the front and add the strap. The body of the bag will slip into the circle *(Illustration 1)*.

Brick Stitch #3

A quick design lesson. The brick stitch can be worked in the round and we'll make the circular band that way. Much of the time, you'll see brick stitch worked flat. The brick stitch has a natural decrease. Every row will automatically have 1 less bead or set of beads than the previous row. Therefore, a flat piece of brick stitch is triangular in shape like the front piece of the body.
To make the diamond shaped back piece, simply work a triangle, flip it over and work another triangle on the bottom *(Illustration 2)*.

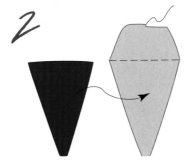

Let's get started. First make the front triangle piece. Pour some of the metallic seed beads into a shallow bowl. Cut a 48" length of thread. Thread the needle with one end. Thread on four beads. Slide them down the thread, leaving the last 12" of thread free. Wrap this end around the index finger of your free hand. You'll pull against this as you tighten the first few stitches.

Row 1 - Now thread the needle back through all four beads. Adjust work into two groups of two beads each *(Illustration 3)*.

String two beads and thread needle back through second group of two beads and the new beads. Now you have three groups of two beads each *(Illustration 4)*.

Continue until you have 21 groups.

Row 2 - String four beads. Notice the loops connecting each group of beads across the top edge of Row 1. Skip the loop just next to the thread and hook the needle under the second loop. Bring needle back up through the last two beads *(Illustration 5)*.

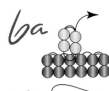

This next step isn't part of the traditional brick stitch, but I use it and offer it to you. Pass the needle back down through the first set of beads, try to catch the first loop of thread, and then bring the needle back up through the second set *(Illustration 6 - 6a)*. This "locks" the first group of beads to the second and keeps it in line with the rest of the row.

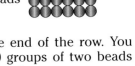

String two beads, hook needle under next loop and bring needle back up through beads *(Illustration 7)*.

Continue to the end of the row. You should have 20 groups of two beads each in this second row.

Rows 3 through 19 - Turn the piece over and work as for Round 2. You will have one less set of beads in each row. Row 19 should have three sets of two beads each. Weave the needle back through several sets of beads to secure the end. Clip the thread *(Illustration 8)*.

Let's face facts. You're going to run out of thread at some point, but there's no need to panic – or to tie a knot! To end a thread, weave up and down through a couple of bead groups on 2 or 3 rounds below. Clip thread end. Cut a 36" length of thread and weave up and down through a couple of bead groups on 2 or 3 rounds to come up out of the last group of beads you added. Weave down to end a thread, weave up to start a new one *(Illustration 9)*.

Weave up to begin a new thread.

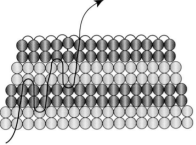

Ready to make the diamond? Pour a few Black seed beads into a shallow bowl. Make a Black triangle just as you did with the metallic beads. When you finish Row 19, weave the needle back down through the diamond so the thread comes out on one end of the bottom row *(Illustration 10)*.

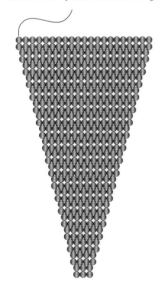

You are going to make the first three rows of this side with single seed beads. Why? This is where the flap folds. And it's much easier to bend single bead rows. Keeping this in mind, you might want to make your stitches slightly loose. Don't overdo it though. Working the first few rows with single beads also makes the piece slightly shorter all around so that the Black flap will be framed with color when the tote is closed.

Continued on page 32

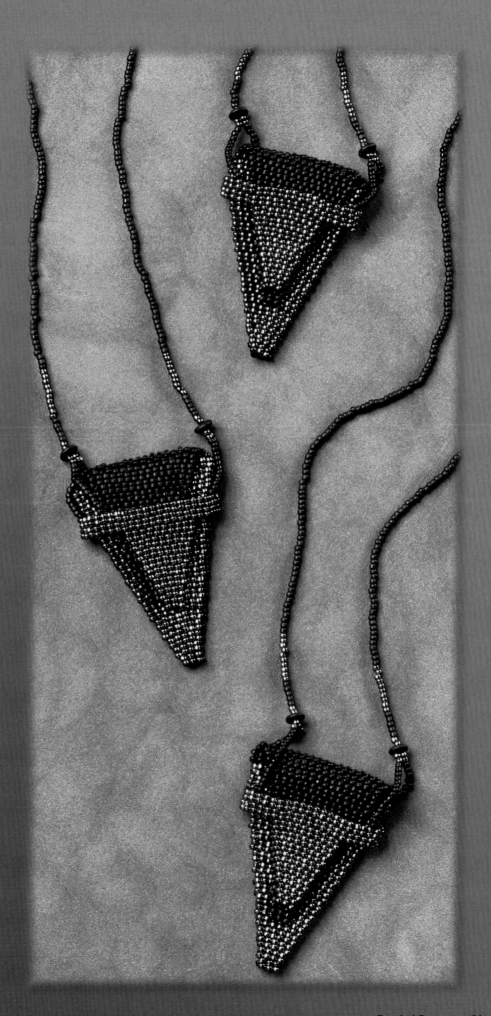

Illustration 11 shows the beading diagram for this side of the diamond. When the diamond is completed, weave the thread back through several rows before clipping the end.

Stitch the pieces together. Thread the needle with 48" of beading thread. Place the triangle over the diamond, aligning rows. Make sure you are using the correct side of the diamond, the one with two bead groups throughout. Stitch the sides together as shown in Illustration 12. Whipstitch the loops of the bottom rows together to close the very bottom point of the bag.

Make the circle.

Row 1 - Using metallic seed beads, thread four beads on 48" of thread and begin making the first row just as you did for the triangle and diamond *(Illustrations 3, 3a, 4)*.
Continue adding groups of two beads until you have a total of 42 groups. Join the first group to the last by running the thread through both groups *(Illustration 13)*.

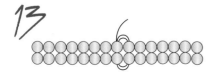

Row 2 - String 4 beads. Skip the loop next to the thread and hook the needle under the second loop. Bring the needle back up through the last two beads *(Illustration 5)*.

Here's your "locking step".
Pass the needle back down through the first set of two beads, catch the skipped loop and then thread the needle back up through the second group *(Illustrations 14 - 14a)*.

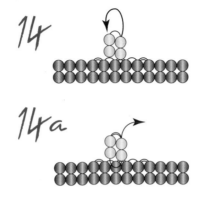

String two more beads. Hook the needle under the next loop and bring it back up through both beads *(Illustration 7)*.
Add groups of two beads around. You'll have 42 groups in this row, too. Circular brick stitch doesn't naturally decrease. Join the first and last groups *(Illustration 15)*.

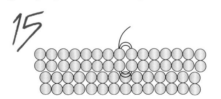

Let's add the diamond to the loop. Work 10 groups of two beads along the circle. Turn the piece over and work 7 rows of flat brick stitch over those 10 groups. The last row should have three groups of two beads *(Illustration 16)*.

Make the strap. Fold the circle in half, centering the diamond – 21 stitches across the front and 21 across the back. Thread 70" of beading thread and weave the end through several

sets of beads to secure. Bring the needle up through the third group from the left on the front of the circle. See Illustration 17 to bead this portion of the strap.

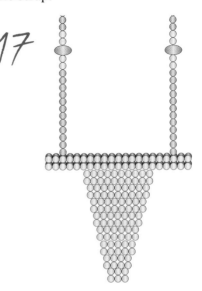

Join the strap to the other side of the circle by bringing the needle back down through the top of the third group from the right side. Weave the thread in and out through several groups. Bring the thread up from the third group from the right on the back of the circle. Thread the first 15 beads and pass the needle back through all the beads on the strap between the two Black disks. Thread 15 more beads and join to the circle at the third group from the left on the back side *(Illustration 18)*. Reinforce the strap by threading back through all the beads once more.

Well done! You've mastered the brick stitch and made yourself a nifty little amulet bag.

Fun and Easy To Make Matchbox Bag

Try your hand at this variation of Ndebele/Herringbone stitch which resembles loomed work… all the beads fall into vertical rows. It's fun and easy to do!

Matchbox Bag size is 1½" wide x 2" high.

Black Bag
MATERIALS: 2 Sterling Silver 4mm round beads • ⅜" wide Sterling Silver pendant • Cardstock for insert • Size B beading thread • Size 12 beading needle
Toho Beads:
• 29 grams 11/0 round matte Black #610

Plum Bag
MATERIALS: • 2 Sterling Silver 4mm round beads • ⅜" wide Sterling Silver pendant • Cardstock for insert • Size B beading thread • Size 12 beading needle
Toho Beads:
• 29 grams 11/0 round matte Bronze Plum #514F

Blue Bag
MATERIALS: 2 Sterling Silver 4mm round beads • ⅜" wide Sterling Silver pendant • Cardstock for insert • Size B beading thread • Size 12 beading needle
Toho Beads:
• 29 grams 11/0 round matte Denim Blue #511F

The Big Picture
You'll be making the bag in three pieces - a circular body and flat bottom and flap. Next, add an insert to help "square" the bag and finally add strap (*Illustration 1*).

Ndebele Variation

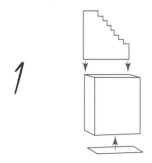

A few notes on Ndebele. Why this stitch? Two reasons: first, we can always use another stitch in our beading repertoire. Secondly, it makes design sense. I wanted to make a square bag – a box. This stitch is perfect. Nice even rows with square edges!

Tension is an important thing to mention at this point. The instructions will tell you to "snug" a bead into place. Pull with a gentle tension until the bead slips into place, don't force it. This stitch is best worked with a little bit of play and a lot of faith. You'll be adding beads to the top row and straightening the beads of the previous row all at the same time. Don't be discouraged if your top row looks a mess, it's supposed to! Eventually, you'll get into the rhythm of the stitch and things will progress quickly from there.

Let's Get Started! Pour some seed beads into a shallow bowl. Cut a 48" length of thread. Thread the needle with one end. Thread on four beads. Slide them down the thread, leaving the last 12" of thread free. Wrap this end around the index finger of your free hand. You'll pull against this as you tighten the first few stitches.

Row 1 - Now thread the needle back through all four beads. Adjust work into two groups of two beads each (*Illustration 2*).

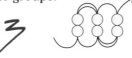

String two beads and thread needle back through second group of two beads and the new beads. Now you have three groups of two beads each (*Illustration 3*). Continue until you have 40 groups.

Join the first and last group by running the thread through both groups as shown in Illustration 4.

Row 2 - Thread two beads. Pass needle down through both beads of the next group (*Illustration 5*).

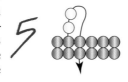

Bring the needle back up through both beads of the third group (*Illustration 6*).

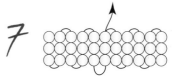

Continue to add two beads with every stitch across the row. When you reach the last stitch, thread the needle back up through the first group (*Illustration 7*).

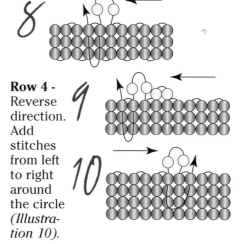

Row 3 - Reverse direction. String two beads, take the needle down through the bead to the left of the thread (a single bead, not a group this time). Come up through the next bead. Continue around (*Illustrations 8 - 9*).

Row 4 - Reverse direction. Add stitches from left to right around the circle (*Illustration 10*).

Rows 5 through 26 - Work as for Rows 3 and 4. Reverse direction with each row. When you have completed row 26, reverse direction and stitch another row without beads. This tidies up the last row of beadwork (*Illustration 11*).

Weave up to begin a new thread.

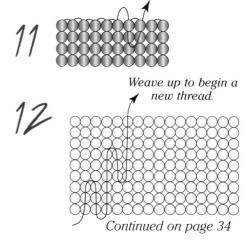

Continued on page 34

Matchbox Ndebele Stitch
Continued from page 33

Let's face facts.
You're going to run out of thread at some point, but there's no need to panic – or to tie a knot! To end a thread, weave up and down through a couple of bead groups on 2 or 3 rounds below. Clip thread end. Cut a 36" length of thread and weave up and down through a couple of bead groups on 2 or 3 rounds to come up out of the last group of beads you added. Weave down to end a thread, weave up to start a new one *(Illustration 12)*.

Let's Make the Bottom Panel! The bottom panel is worked flat. The direction of the stitches still changes with every row. But we'll simply turn the piece over and continue to work from left to right. (We are so sneaky!)

Row 1 - Make a ladder as for Row 1 of the body with 5 sets of two beads *(Illustration 13)*.

Row 2 - Flip the ladder over so you're working from left to right. Make two stitches through the bead groups of Row 1 *(Illustrations 14 - 15)*.

Row 3 - Flip the piece over so you're working from left to right. String 3 beads and make the first stitch of the row as shown in Illustration 16. Notice we are now going through single beads instead of groups.

 String two beads and make the next stitch *(Illustration 17)*.

Row 4 - Flip the piece over so you're working from left to right. String 3 beads and make the first stitch of the row as shown in *Illustration 18*.

Rows 5 through 19 - Continue to work the panel for a total of 19 rows. Remember to work a 20th row without beads to tidy up Row 19.

Join the panel to the bag. Thread your beading needle with 24" of thread. Weave the end through several rows of the bag and come up out of a bead on the bottom edge. Stitch one short side of the panel to the bottom of the bag as shown in Illustration 19. NOTE: As you stitch, try to keep the panel resting on top of the bottom row of beads.